INVESTING IN REAL ESTATE

A Guide for Beginners

Philipp Frühwirth

CONTENTS

INTRODUCTION TO REAL ESTATE INVESTING

Real estate investing is a popular and lucrative way to build wealth, generate passive income, and create a secure financial future. However, some people are hesitant to get started in real estate investing because it can seem intimidating and complex. In this chapter, we will introduce you to the world of real estate investing, its benefits, and some basic principles to get you started.

Real estate investing refers to the buying, owning, managing, renting, and/or selling of real estate for financial gain. Real estate assets can include residential properties like single-family homes, townhouses, and apartments, as well as commercial properties such as office buildings, retail spaces, and warehouses. Investors may choose to buy and hold a property for the long term or flip it for a quick profit.

One of the primary benefits of real estate investing is the potential for significant returns. When done correctly, real estate investments can generate impressive profit margins, including rental income and appreciation in property value. According to Forbes, real estate has outperformed the stock market and other investment options in terms of returns over the past two decades.

Compared to other types of investments, real estate investing can also offer greater control and stability. As a real estate investor, you have the power to make strategic decisions about buying, holding or selling a property, and can control many of the variables that influence its success. Real estate investments can also provide tax benefits, including deductions for property expenses and depreciation of buildings.

Before jumping into real estate investing, it's important to have a well-defined plan, including your goals, target market, and investment strategy. Creating a solid plan will help you stay organized and focused, and will better prepare you for success in this competitive market.

Real estate investing can seem complex, but it's important to remember that it's ultimately about people and relationships. You'll need to build connections with real estate agents, investors, lenders, property managers, and other professionals who can help you achieve your investment goals.

In conclusion, real estate investing can be a great way to build wealth and secure your financial future. With the potential for significant returns, greater control, and tax benefits, real estate investing is worth considering as a viable option for investors of all levels. In the following chapters, we will explore different types of real estate investments, financing options, and key strategies for success.

BENEFITS OF REAL ESTATE INVESTING

Real estate investing has always been a popular way to build wealth and secure long-term financial prosperity. With the potential for high returns and multiple investment opportunities, real estate is considered as one of the most secure and profitable investment choices. Many people choose real estate investments as their primary source of income or as a supplementary income stream.

Here are some of the significant benefits of real estate investing:

1. Steady cash flow

One of the main advantages of real estate investing is the ability to generate consistent cash flow by owning rental properties. Rent collected from tenants provides regular income with the potential for long-term capital appreciation. This helps to create a steady stream of passive income for property owners, allowing them to invest in other ventures or enjoy the fruits of their labor.

2. Long-term capital appreciation

Real estate is known for its significant long-term appreciation potential. Property values typically increase over time, meaning that an investor who buys a property today at a reasonable price can sell it for a much higher price in the future. This long-term appreciation can be a powerful way to build wealth over time and secure your financial future.

3. Tax benefits

Real estate properties come with various tax advantages that can help reduce your income taxes. Rental income is often taxed at favorable rates compared to other forms of income, and investors can also take advantage of depreciation deductions to further lower their taxable income. Moreover, real estate investors also have access to capital gains tax benefits.

4. Diversification

Investing in real estate can be an excellent way to diversify an investment portfolio. Real estate properties are typically less volatile than stocks and other types of investments, making them an attractive option for those seeking to balance their portfolio and minimize risk.

5. Hedge against inflation

Real estate investments can serve as a hedge against inflation, as property values tend to rise in tandem with inflation. This means that the value of your investment is protected against the rising cost of living and helps to maintain purchasing power over the long-term.

In conclusion, real estate investing offers an attractive combination of steady cash flow, long-term capital appreciation potential, tax savings, diversification, and protection against inflation. These are just a few of the reasons why investors should consider incorporating real estate into their investment portfolio.

TYPES OF REAL ESTATE INVESTMENTS

Real estate investing is a great way to build wealth and achieve financial independence. One of the key benefits of real estate investing is that there are many different types of investments to choose from depending on your goals and risk tolerance. Here are some of the most common types of real estate investments:

1. Rental Properties

Rental properties are perhaps the most popular type of real estate investment. With rental properties, you buy a property and rent it out to tenants. The rent you receive each month can provide you with regular income, and as the property increases in value over time, you can sell it for a profit.

2. Commercial Properties

Commercial properties are another popular type of real estate investment. Commercial properties can include office buildings, retail spaces, warehouses, and more. These types of properties can provide long-term tenants and reliable income for investors.

3. Real Estate Investment Trusts (REITs)

REITs are essentially dividend-paying stocks that invest in real estate. REITs offer investors the chance to invest in real estate without the hassle of becoming a landlord or needing a large amount of capital to get started.

4. Real Estate Crowdfunding

Real estate crowdfunding involves pooling money with other investors to invest in a real estate project. Investors typically earn returns through interest payments or a percentage of the profits.

5. House Flipping

House flipping involves buying a property, fixing it up, and selling it for a profit. This type of investment can be very lucrative but also requires a significant amount of work, expertise, and risk.

6. Real Estate Development

Lastly, real estate development involves buying land and building new properties on it. This type of investment can be very profitable but also involves a significant amount of capital and risk.

In conclusion, there are many different types of real estate investments to choose from depending on your goals and risk tolerance. It's important to do your research, assess your financial situation, and choose the right type of real estate investment for you.

CREATING A REAL ESTATE INVESTMENT PLAN

Real estate investing is a lucrative industry. It offers investors a wide range of opportunities to earn consistent cash flow, build wealth, and achieve long-term financial success. However, success in real estate investing takes preparation, hard work, and a well-thought-out plan. Here are some steps to help you create a realistic real estate investment plan.

1. Set specific investment goals

Before you begin investing in real estate, you need to know what you want to achieve. Your investment goals may include generating passive income through rentals, flipping properties for a quick profit, or building long-term wealth through appreciation. Once you identify your goals, quantify them. For example, you may set a goal of earning $30,000 per year in rental income or flipping three properties per year.

2. Determine your investment budget

Real estate investing can require a significant amount of capital, so you need to determine how much you are willing to invest. Evaluate your current financial situation, including your income, debts, and other expenses to determine how much you can afford to invest in real estate. Your budget should also include potential down payments, closing costs, renovation expenses, and any other associated costs.

3. Research your investment options

Before investing your hard-earned money, it's necessary to research the different types of real estate investments available.

These include single-family homes, multi-unit properties, commercial properties, and more.

You should also consider the location, rental yield, and vacancy rates in the area you are considering. By doing so, you can identify the most suitable investment for your budget and goals.

4. Create a detailed investment plan

Once you've identified your investment goals, budget, and target property, you need to create a detailed investment plan. Your plan should outline the steps you need to take to succeed in your investment venture, including timelines, financial projections, marketing strategies, and any other necessary details.

5. Implement your plan

The final step is to implement your real estate investment plan. You'll need to work diligently to achieve your investment goals, and you should regularly track your progress. Be prepared to make adjustments along the way as necessary.

In conclusion, creating a real estate investment plan is a necessary step to succeed in the industry. By setting specific investment goals, creating a budget, researching your investment options, and creating a detailed plan, you can increase your chances of achieving long-term financial success through real estate investing.

ANALYZING REAL ESTATE INVESTMENT OPPORTUNITIES

Real estate investment is a great way to generate wealth over time. However, investing in real estate is not without risks. Wise real estate investors take considerable time to research and analyze potential investment opportunities, doing their due diligence to ensure a profitable investment. Analyzing a real estate investment opportunity involves evaluating several factors to determine if the investment is worth the risk. Here are some factors to consider.

Location

Location is the most critical factor when it comes to real estate investing. A property's location can determine its value and how profitable it is for investment purposes. Before you invest in any real estate, research the area thoroughly. Look at the local economy, job market, and population growth. Invest in locations where there is high demand for housing and where real estate appreciation is expected to be high.

Property Condition

When analyzing a real estate investment opportunity, you need to assess the property's condition. Conducting a thorough inspection is crucial to determining the property's value. If you are buying a fixer-upper, hire a professional inspector to identify all issues and determine repair costs. Ensure the expected cost of repairs, renovations, and maintenance is well within your budget.

Neighborhood Crime Rate

Safety is another important factor to consider. Analyze the crime rate in the neighborhood where you plan on investing. The safety of your tenants is paramount, and properties located in high crime rate areas are difficult to rent out, reducing profitability.

Market Trends

Real estate markets fluctuate, and it's essential to keep a close eye on trends to make informed investment decisions. Analyzing market trends will help you evaluate if the investment opportunity will generate profits in the long term.

Rental Demand

If you plan on investing in rental properties, evaluate the demand for rental housing in the area. Look at how quickly similar properties are renting out, rental prices, and tenant retention rates. If demand for rental housing is high, the chances are that your property will remain rented and generate cash flow.

Financing Options

Analyzing investment opportunities should also involve exploring financing options. Many investors finance their investments through mortgages, hard money loans, and other financing options. Evaluate financing options you can leverage to construct a feasible investment strategy that aligns with your financial goals.

Conclusion

Analyzing real estate investment opportunities requires significant research and attention to detail. Consider an investment in real estate as a business opportunity rather than a hobby. Identifying factors like location, property condition, market trends, rental demand, and financing options is key to making successful investment decisions. Ensure you work with trusted and reputable real estate agents, inspectors, and other professionals.

FINANCING REAL ESTATE INVESTMENTS

Real estate investing can be a lucrative way to create long-term wealth, but it requires money to get started. Many investors need financing to purchase their first or subsequent properties. There are several financing options available for real estate investors, including traditional mortgages, private loans, hard money loans, and more.

Traditional Mortgages
Conventional mortgages are loans that investors obtain from banks, credit unions, or mortgage lenders. These loans are best for investors with a good credit score, steady income, and a significant down payment. To be approved for a conventional mortgage, the lender requires the investor to meet certain qualifications, such as a minimum credit score, income levels, and debt-to-income ratios. These loans typically offer the lowest interest rates, with terms ranging from 15 to 30 years.

Private Loans
Some investors may have trouble securing traditional financing for their real estate investments. Private loans are an alternative financing option in which the investor borrows money from a private individual or company instead of a bank. Private loans tend to be more flexible and can be customized to meet the specific needs of the investor. In general, private loans have higher interest rates and shorter terms than conventional mortgages.

Hard Money Loans
Hard money loans are short-term loans that are secured by the property being purchased. These types of loans are often used by investors who cannot obtain traditional financing or private

loans. Hard money lenders are usually private individuals or small lending firms who provide financing based on the value of the property rather than the creditworthiness of the borrower. A hard money loan typically has a higher interest rate and may have additional fees, such as origination fees and points.

Seller Financing

In some cases, the property seller may be willing to finance the purchase for the buyer. This can be a good financing option for investors who have trouble obtaining traditional financing or private loans. The terms of seller financing can vary widely, but usually, it involves the seller holding a promissory note for the purchase price of the property, with the buyer making payments to the seller over a certain period of time.

Crowdfunding

Crowdfunding has become a popular way to finance real estate investments. In this process, multiple investors pool their funds together to purchase a property. Crowdfunding can either be done through a platform-specific for real estate investing or through social media channels. This type of funding allows investors to gain access to larger capital amounts to conduct investments they would not be able to afford on their funds.

In conclusion, financing is a crucial component in real estate investing. Understanding the various financing options can help investors select the best financing option for their investment style, situation, and goals. Before selecting the financing option suits best, consult with a financial advisor to get professional guidance.

BUILDING A REAL ESTATE INVESTMENT PORTFOLIO

Building a real estate investment portfolio is all about creating a diverse range of investments that match your goals, risk tolerance, and budget. It involves deciding what type of properties or investments you want to own and then acquiring them over time. Here are the key steps to follow to build your real estate investment portfolio:

1. Determine your investment goals and risk tolerance. Before you start investing, it is essential to understand what you want to achieve and how much risk you are willing to take. Your investment goal can be capital appreciation, passive income or both. Your risk tolerance is a measure of how much you are comfortable with investing in different types of properties, and market cycles.

2. Choose an investment strategy. There are many strategies you can use to build your real estate investment portfolio, including long-term rentals, student housing, vacation rental, fix and flip, and commercial real estate. Each strategy has its unique characteristics and investment criteria.

3. Find the right properties. After establishing your investment strategy, start looking for properties that meet your criteria. Look for properties that have strong potential for appreciation, have long-term rental potential, or other key factors that fit your investment goals. Be thorough in your research and due diligence to avoid investing in problematic properties.

4. Analyze the financials. In addition to researching properties, you also need to perform a thorough financial analysis. Consider

the purchase price, development costs if any, property taxes, interest rates, insurance costs, maintenance and repairs, and other expenses that impact your bottom line.

5. Finance your investments. Financing your investments through different options like loans or private equity is another crucial step. You should always minimize your risk by using the right financing strategies.

6. Monitor your investments. After acquiring properties, you must become a qualified property manager. You should keep track of your properties' day-to-day operations, as well as monitoring their financial progress. Seek professional assistance from established property management firms.

Building a real estate investment portfolio is a long-term endeavor that requires patience, discipline, and a strong commitment to your investment goals. By following the above steps, you can effectively create an investment portfolio that will help you grow your wealth, generate passive income, and achieve financial freedom.

MANAGING PROPERTIES AS AN INVESTOR

As a real estate investor, managing your properties effectively is crucial to success. From screening tenants to maintaining the property, good management practices can help maximize your profits and minimize your risks.

Here are some essential tips for managing your properties as an investor:

1. Find Good Tenants - Finding the right tenants who can pay the rent on time and take good care of your property is crucial. You can screen tenants by running background checks, reviewing rental history, and verifying employment and income.

2. Set Clear Expectations - Before renting out a property, make sure you lay out clear guidelines and expectations for tenants. This includes rental payment due dates, maintenance responsibilities, and consequences for breaking lease agreements.

3. Regular Maintenance - Keeping up with maintenance can prevent small, easily fixable issues from turning into larger, more expensive ones. Regular maintenance can also help you retain good tenants and keep your property in top condition.

4. Build Good Relationships - Build a good relationship with your tenants by responding to their requests promptly and being courteous and professional in your dealings with them. This can lead to longer tenancies and positive word-of-mouth advertising.

5. Track Expenses - Tracking expenses such as repairs, tax payments, and mortgage payments can help you stay on top of your cash flow and make informed decisions about future

investments.

6. Keep Up With Local Laws - Familiarize yourself with the landlord-tenant laws and regulations in your state and city. This can help you avoid costly legal issues and stay compliant with local laws.

7. Consider Hiring a Property Manager - If you have multiple properties or lack the time or expertise to manage your properties effectively, consider hiring a property manager. They can help you handle tenant relations, manage maintenance, and take care of administrative tasks.

In conclusion, managing your properties effectively is crucial for any real estate investor. By following these tips, you can help maximize your profits and minimize your risks.

ESSENTIAL REAL ESTATE INVESTMENT TOOLS AND RESOURCES

Real estate investing has grown significantly in popularity over the years, and as a result, a plethora of tools and resources have emerged to aid investors in managing their endeavors. From tools that help investors calculate ROI to online communities where investors share their experiences and advice, the world of real estate investing tools and resources is vast and ever-evolving. In this chapter, we'll explore some of the essential tools and resources that every real estate investor should know about.

1. Analytical Tools
Analytical tools are essential to real estate investing, especially when it comes to analyzing investment opportunities. These tools help investors make informed decisions based on factors like market trends, local demographics, and property valuations. Some of the most popular analytical tools include online platforms like LoopNet, Reonomy, and Real Data.

2. Investment Management Software
One crucial aspect of real estate investing is keeping track of your investments effectively. Investment management software tools like ARGUS Enterprise and Yardi can assist investors in tracking income and expenses, calculating ROI, and managing tenants.

3. Property Management Software
Investors who choose to manage their properties in-house can benefit from using software tools that simplify the entire process of property management. These tools provide features like tenant tracking, maintenance requests routing, and rent collection. Some

popular options include Appfolio, Propertyware, and Buildium.

4. Online Forums and Communities

Finally, online communities and forums provide real estate investors with a wealth of resources when it comes to learning about the industry, receiving advice, and networking with other investors. BiggerPockets, Reddit, and ActiveRain are just a few examples of online communities that bring together investors, contractors, and service providers.

In conclusion, real estate investing comes with its unique set of challenges that require suitable tools and resources to tackle them. While the number of options can be overwhelming, investors need to research and select those resources that align with their investment goals and strategies to enable them to achieve success in this lucrative but challenging field.

DIVERSIFYING YOUR REAL ESTATE INVESTMENT PORTFOLIO

Like any other investment, real estate can be unpredictable, which underlines the importance of diversification. Diversifying your real estate investment portfolio can help you manage risks and create opportunities for increased returns. Here are some tips to help you diversify your real estate investment portfolio:

1. Invest in Different Types of Properties

A simple way to diversify your investment portfolio is to invest in different types of properties. For instance, you may own rental properties, commercial properties, or fix-and-flip properties. By spreading your investments across different types of properties, you can mitigate the risk of relying on one type.

2. Invest in Different Geographic Areas

Investing in different areas can protect you from the potential negative effects of an economic downturn in a particular area. For example, you may own properties in different cities, states, or even countries. Real estate markets can differ vastly in the level of competition, cash flow potential, and tenant demographics, so investing in multiple areas can help you capitalize on the best opportunities in each region.

3. Invest in Different Real Estate Niches

When investing in real estate, there are many sub-niches to explore. For instance, you may invest in student housing, vacation rentals, self-storage, or mobile home parks. By investing in different niches, you can minimize your risk by diversifying your investments in properties that have unique cash flow drivers.

4. Invest in REITs or Real Estate Mutual Funds

Real Estate Investment Trusts (REITs) and real estate mutual funds allow you to invest in different types of properties without actually buying real estate. REITs are companies that own and operate income-generating real estate properties like hotels, offices, and residential apartments. By investing in these companies, you can benefit from professional management and the returns generated by the properties in their portfolio.

5. Invest in Real Estate Crowdfunding

Real estate crowdfunding platforms, like Fundrise or RealtyMogul, allow you to invest in real estate projects alongside other investors. This allows you to diversify your investments, even with a small amount of money. Real estate crowdfunding also allows you to invest in diverse projects, which can also increase your returns.

In conclusion, diversification is key to managing risk, and it is prudent to apply this principle to your real estate investment portfolio. By diversifying your portfolio, you will enjoy the benefits of multiple streams of income and be better positioned to weather market uncertainties.

TAX CONSIDERATIONS FOR REAL ESTATE INVESTORS

One of the significant advantages of investing in real estate is the tax benefits. There are several tax advantages that real estate investors can enjoy when they make a property investment.

Depreciation is one of the primary tax benefits that investors can enjoy. Depreciation is a tax deduction that allows investors to deduct a portion of the property's purchase price over time. The value of the property is divided by 27.5 years, and the deduction is taken annually. It means that over the years, investors can collect a substantial amount in depreciation deductions, which they can offset against their taxable income.

Another tax benefit available to real estate investors is the 1031 exchange. It is a provision in the tax code that allows investors to sell an investment property and reinvest the proceeds into a similar investment property within a specified period, usually 180 days. In other words, it enables an investor to avoid paying capital gains taxes when selling a property, provided they reinvest the proceeds in another property.

Real estate investors can also receive a tax deduction on their mortgage interest payments. This tax deduction could be a significant benefit for investors with multiple properties, as interest payments can add up and represent a substantial amount.

The cost of repairs and maintenance can also be tax-deductible. It means that any expenses incurred in making repairs on rental properties can be written off as an expense in the current year.

Finally, investors can also benefit from tax deductions on their property taxes. This deduction will depend on individual circumstances and the tax laws in the investor's location.

As real estate investors consider the tax benefits available to them, it is essential to work with a competent tax professional to ensure they maximize their deductions and minimize their tax obligations. It might also be essential to adopt a tax strategy and plan that aligns with their overall real estate investment plans and goals.

In conclusion, real estate investing presents significant tax benefits for those willing to do their due diligence and take advantage of them. They can create a tax strategy in collaboration with their tax professional to minimize their tax obligations and help them achieve their investment goals.

THE PROS AND CONS OF COMMERCIAL AND RESIDENTIAL REAL ESTATE INVESTMENTS

When it comes to real estate investment, one of the crucial decisions you need to make is choosing between commercial and residential properties. Both options offer different advantages and disadvantages, and understanding them can help you make an informed investment decision. In this chapter, we will discuss the pros and cons of commercial and residential real estate investments.

Pros of Commercial Real Estate Investments

1. Higher Returns: Commercial properties typically have higher returns compared to residential properties due to longer leases, increased revenue streams, and higher rental rates.

2. Professional Relationships: Commercial real estate investments offer the opportunity to build relationships with other investors, tenants, and brokers, which can lead to more lucrative deals.

3. Flexibility: Investors in commercial real estate can choose from various types of properties, including offices, warehouses, retail spaces, and even hotels, offering flexibility in investment choices.

4. Fewer Tenant Issues: Commercial properties usually have long-term, stable tenants, such as businesses, that usually sign long-term lease agreements. This means fewer tenant issues like evictions or unpaid rent compared to residential properties.

Cons of Commercial Real Estate Investments

1. Higher Cost: Commercial properties are usually expensive compared to residential, and most of the time, you will need to finance your investment with a commercial loan, which can come with higher interest rates.

2. High Entry Barriers: Investing in commercial real estate requires a large initial investment, making it difficult for beginners to enter the market.

3. Longer Lease Periods: Without regular lease turnover, commercial real estate can be challenging to manage, as tenants sign long-term leases of several years.

Pros of Residential Real Estate Investments

1. Lower Cost: The cost of residential real estate is typically lower compared to commercial properties, making it easier for beginners to enter the market.

2. Increased Flexibility: Residential property investments can offer more flexibility, including rental properties and fix-and-flip opportunities.

3. Higher Demand: Rental properties and homes are always in high demand, especially in suburban locations, making occupancy rates generally higher.

4. Easier to Manage: Managing residential properties is usually less challenging as they are typically less complicated than commercial buildings.

Cons of Residential Real Estate Investments

1. Less Stable: Compared to commercial real estate, residential properties can have a lot of tenant turnover, which can lead to long periods of vacancy or difficulty taking care of the property.

2. Lower Rental Income: Rental income from residential properties is usually lower compared to commercial buildings, meaning lower ROI and longer investment payback periods.

3. Emergencies and Repairs: Residential properties can be more prone to emergencies, including water and electrical issues that can require immediate repairs.

Overall, both commercial and residential real estate investments have their benefits and drawbacks. Knowing which investment type is right for you depends on your investment goals, budget, market trends, and risk appetite.

TIPS FOR INVESTING IN RENTAL PROPERTIES

Investing in rental properties can be a lucrative way to generate passive income and build wealth over time. However, it is important to approach this type of investment with the right strategy and mindset. Here are some tips for investing in rental properties:

1. Determine Your Goals: Before you start searching for properties, it's important to determine your investment goals. Are you looking for a long-term investment or a short-term profit? What kind of cash flow are you looking to generate? These questions will help you determine the type of property you should invest in.

2. Research the Market: Conduct thorough market research to identify the best locations to invest in. Look for areas with strong rental demand and lower vacancy rates. This will ensure that your property is occupied quickly and generates consistent cash flow.

3. Analyze Potential Properties: Once you've identified a potential property, make sure to conduct a thorough analysis to determine its profitability. Consider the property's location, condition, and amenities. Run the numbers and make sure there's enough cash flow to cover expenses and generate a profit.

4. Screen Tenants Carefully: Good tenants are the key to a successful rental property investment. Make sure to conduct thorough background and credit checks on potential tenants. Look for tenants who have a steady income, good credit history, and a clean rental record.

5. Set the Right Rent: Setting the right rent price is crucial for rental property investing. You want to charge enough to cover

your expenses and generate a profit, but you also don't want to price yourself out of the market. Conduct market research to determine the average rent prices in the area and set your rent accordingly.

6. Hire a Property Manager: As a rental property investor, you may not have the time or expertise to manage the property yourself. Consider hiring a property manager to take care of day-to-day operations, such as tenant screening, rent collection, and maintenance.

7. Stay Compliant with the Law: Make sure to stay compliant with all local and state laws regarding rental properties. This includes things like fair housing laws, rental property inspections, and eviction procedures. Staying compliant will help you avoid costly fines and legal issues.

Investing in rental properties can be a great way to generate passive income and build long-term wealth. By approaching this type of investment with the right strategy and mindset, you can set yourself up for success and achieve your financial goals.

FLIPPING PROPERTIES
FOR PROFIT

Flipping properties, or buying a property with the intention of selling it quickly at a profit, is a strategy that has become increasingly popular in recent years. If done correctly, flipping properties can be a lucrative way to invest in real estate. Here are some tips to help you successfully flip properties for profit.

1. Research the Market
Before you start flipping properties, you need to do your research. Study the real estate market in the area where you plan to invest. Look at property prices, trends and the demand for properties. Identify the types of properties that are in high demand and have low supply. Your aim is to buy property below the market price and sell it for a profit.

2. Know Your Budget
You need to have a clear budget in mind before you start flipping properties. Consider the cost of buying the property, repair costs and other expenses such as taxes, permits, and insurance. Create a spreadsheet for each property that you are considering and calculate the potential profit margin. Your goal should be to make a profit of at least 15% of the property's value.

3. Work with Professionals
You cannot flip a property by yourself. You need to work with a team of professionals including real estate agents, contractors, and lawyers. Choose professionals that have a good reputation and experience in flipping properties. Your team will provide you with the necessary knowledge and support throughout the flipping process.

4. Focus on Cosmetic Changes

When flipping properties, you want to focus on cosmetic changes that will enhance the property's aesthetic appeal. You do not want to invest too much money into features that will not increase the property's value. Some cosmetic changes you can make include painting the walls, adding new fixtures, and updating appliances.

5. Pricing Strategies

Pricing the property correctly is important for the resale process. You do not want to price it too high and deter potential buyers, or price it too low and leave money on the table. Look at the market trends and comparable properties in the area. Price the property competitively to attract buyers and make a profit.

6. Timing is Key

Timing is critical when it comes to flipping properties. You need to sell the property at the right time to maximize your profit. The real estate market is constantly changing, so it is important to pay attention to trends and sell the property when the market is strong.

Flipping properties can be a lucrative way to invest in real estate. It requires careful research, planning, and execution to make a profit. By following these tips, you can successfully flip properties for profit.

LONG-TERM INVESTING STRATEGIES IN REAL ESTATE

While some investors prefer to buy a property, flip it for a quick profit, and move on to the next deal, others take a long-term approach to real estate investing. This strategy involves holding onto a property for a period of years, collecting rental income, and benefiting from appreciation over time. Long-term investing in real estate can be a great way to build wealth, but it's important to have a plan in place.

Here are some tips for long-term investing strategies in real estate:

1. Buy and hold: This is the most common long-term investment strategy in real estate. The idea is to purchase a property, preferably at a discount, and hold onto it for a number of years while renting it out to tenants. Over time, the property will likely appreciate in value, while you earn rental income along the way.

2. Focus on cash flow: When investing for the long-term, it's important to choose properties that generate positive cash flow. This means that the rental income covers all of the property expenses, including mortgage payments, taxes, and maintenance costs. Positive cash flow ensures that the property can be maintained and serviced without dipping into your own savings.

3. Be patient: Long-term real estate investing requires patience. It takes time for a property to appreciate in value and for rental income to pay off. Investors shouldn't expect to get rich overnight. But with a solid investment plan, a property that generates positive cash flow, and some patience, the returns can be substantial.

4. Location is key: Investing in the right location is crucial

for long-term success. Areas that are experiencing population growth, job growth, and other positive economic indicators tend to be good choices. Look for markets that are stable and have a strong track record of appreciation.

5. Diversify your portfolio: Another key to long-term success in real estate investing is to diversify your portfolio. Don't put all of your eggs in one basket – invest in different property types and geographic areas to spread your risk.

6. Use leverage wisely: Borrowing money to invest in real estate can be a smart strategy, but only if you use leverage wisely. Make sure you have a solid plan in place for paying off any loans and avoid taking on too much debt.

7. Don't let emotions cloud your judgment: Finally, it's important to take a rational, analytical approach to real estate investing. Don't let emotions cloud your judgment or cause you to make impulsive decisions. Stick to your investment plan and make decisions based on solid data and analysis.

In conclusion, long-term investing strategies in real estate can be a great way to build wealth over time. By focusing on cash flow, choosing the right location, diversifying your portfolio, and using leverage wisely, investors can find success in this strategy. However, patience and a rational, analytical approach are also key to long-term success in real estate investing.

REAL ESTATE INVESTMENT MISTAKES TO AVOID

Real estate investing is not as easy as it may seem. It is filled with challenging decisions and risks but can be rewarding when done correctly. That said, there are many common real estate investment mistakes that investors tend to make. In this chapter, we will discuss some of these mistakes and how you can avoid them.

1. Lack of planning: One of the major mistakes that many investors make is neglecting the importance of creating a comprehensive plan before investing. Before investing, it is important to identify your goals, research markets, decide on an investment strategy, and anticipate potential challenges.

2. Overpaying for properties: Overpaying for properties is one of the most common mistakes investors make. It is important to have an accurate appraisal or inspection to determine the property's value to ensure that you are not overpaying.

3. Not conducting proper market research: Investing in a property in the wrong market can lead to unfavorable returns. Proper market research will help you identify the potential risks, opportunities, and trends of the area.

4. Ignoring property management: Successful real estate investment does not end at the purchase of a property. Property management is important for maintaining the property's value, ensuring that it attracts tenants, and complying with regulations.

5. Lack of due diligence: Conducting due diligence involves researching the property, looking for legal or environmental issues, reviewing relevant financial statements, and more. Not

conducting sufficient due diligence can lead to unpleasant surprises after the purchase.

6. Over-leveraging: Leverage is a powerful tool for real estate investment, but it can become a liability when over-utilized. Over-leveraging can lead to increased debt, interest payments, and risk when the market declines.

7. Neglecting to consider tax consequences: Forgetting about the tax implications of your investment can lead to significant potential liability. It is important to work with a financial professional to implement tax-reducing strategies.

8. Emotional investing: Treating real estate investing as a business is important because it allows for objective decision-making. Making decisions based on emotion or rushing to invest can lead to mistakes and losses.

9. Failing to anticipate unexpected expenses: Unexpected expenses are common in property ownership, and not anticipating them can strain your investment. It is important to have a reserve fund to cover these expenses.

10. Lack of diversification: Investing all of your funds in a single property type or location can lead to a higher risk of loss. By diversifying your investments, you spread the risk, making it less likely that a single investment will take down your entire portfolio.

In conclusion, real estate investment mistakes can be costly and should be avoided by careful planning, conducting due diligence, managing your properties, diversifying your portfolio, and seeking professional advice when needed.

THE FUTURE OF REAL ESTATE INVESTING

Real estate investing has been a lucrative way to build wealth for many years. With the rise of technology and the changing landscape of the industry, the future of real estate investing is looking very promising. In this chapter, we will explore some of the trends and changes that will shape the future of real estate investing.

1. Increased use of technology – Technology has been rapidly changing the real estate landscape in recent years. The use of blockchain and smart contracts is already disrupting the way real estate transactions are conducted. As the technology continues to advance, we can expect to see more automation and digitization.

2. Growth of alternative investments – Real estate crowdfunding and real estate investment trusts (REITs) are two examples of alternative ways to invest in real estate. These platforms allow for increased diversification and access to real estate investments for smaller investors.

3. Focus on sustainability – As the world becomes more environmentally conscious, sustainable buildings and developments will become more popular. Investors who are able to recognize the potential in sustainable projects will position themselves for success in the future.

4. Emphasis on social responsibility – Similar to sustainability, investors who prioritize social responsibility will have an advantage in the years to come. Investing in properties that offer affordable housing or that are designed to improve the surrounding community will become more valuable.

5. Adaptation to changing demographics – The aging population and rising number of millennials in the market will shift the demand for different types of properties. Investors who are able to recognize and adapt to these changes will reap the benefits.

6. Rise of international investments – With globalisation and the unprecedented level of access to information, real estate investments will become more global. An increasing number of investors will seek opportunities in emerging markets or even diversify their portfolio with overseas assets.

7. Commercial-to-residential development – Changes in the way people work is leading to decreased demand for commercial spaces such as offices and increased demand for residential spaces. Investors may take advantage of this shift and convert older offices into apartments.

Although the future is bright for real estate investing, it is important to note that challenges may arise too. Evolving technologies, market forces and upcoming economic changes will require adaptability and strategic thinking from investors. Yet by paying attention to forecast and identifying potential investment opportunities, it is quite possible to establish a prosperous, long-term investment in this exciting and profitable industry.

MAXIMIZING YOUR REAL ESTATE INVESTMENT PROFITS

If you're interested in real estate investment, it's important to understand that you can't just purchase a property and expect to make a fortune overnight. Maximizing your profits requires a combination of strategic planning, marketing, and hard work. Here are some tips to help you maximize your real estate investment profits.

1. Choose Your Investment Properties Wisely: One of the most crucial factors that determine your success in real estate investment is the choice of property type. Be sure that you choose investment properties that are in high-demand areas, well-situated and located near essential amenities such as schools, transportation, healthcare facilities, and entertainment facilities.

2. Improve Your Property: Once you own a property, look for ways to improve it. This can be done in a variety of ways, from updating the kitchen or bathroom to investing in energy-efficient upgrades. The more attractive and functional your property is, the more likely it is to attract tenants or buyers.

3. Be Upfront with Your Tenants: Communication is key! Be upfront with your tenants from the beginning about any necessary terms and conditions that must be met to keep the property suitable for the next occupant. Let your tenants know that you take care of the property and that you expect the same from them.

4. Keep Your Expenses Low: Keep your expenses low by avoiding high-interest loans, managing related expenses and avoiding costly renovations that do not generate an increase in value.

5. Hire a Professional: In order to truly maximize your returns, you may want to consider hiring a professional property manager to handle your investments. Not only do they have the expertise to handle issues quickly and efficiently, but they also have access to valuable contacts in the industry which can lead to better investment opportunities.

6. Stay Educated: Always try and learn something new about real estate investment. Stay ahead of the curve by continuing to learn about new trends and strategies as they emerge.

By following these tips, you'll be well on your way to maximizing your real estate investment profits, securing your financial future, and living the lifestyle you deserve.

CONCLUSION AND FINAL THOUGHTS FOR REAL ESTATE INVESTORS.

Real estate investing refers to the process of purchasing, managing, owning, and selling properties to earn profits. Investing in real estate is an excellent way to build wealth, generate passive income and gain financial freedom. Real estate investments come in different forms such as commercial, residential, and industrial properties, which can provide investors with several benefits.

Real estate investment provides a way for investors to potentially earn higher returns than traditional investments, such as bonds and stocks. Moreover, unlike these investments that offer only one source of income, real estate investments often have numerous income streams, such as rental income, capital gains, and appreciation.

Investing in real estate also provides a sense of security since real estate assets are tangible and have intrinsic value. Real estate properties can serve as a hedge against inflation, since rental income and property value tend to increase over time at a faster rate than the average inflation rate.

Furthermore, real estate investing is an excellent way to diversify an investment portfolio, thereby reducing the overall risk of an investment strategy. This is because property values do not move in tandem with the stock market, bonds, and other investments, and fluctuations in the value of one type of asset may not affect the performance of other asset classes.

Finally, real estate investment provides several tax benefits, including depreciation deductions, mortgage interest deductions, and Section 1031 exchanges that allow investors to defer capital gains tax on the sale of a property.

In conclusion, real estate investing is a lucrative, sustainable, and relatively safe investment option that offers several benefits to investors. Real estate investing can help individuals to accumulate wealth, generate passive income, and attain financial freedom. However, success in real estate investing requires careful planning, keen analysis of investment opportunities, and a willingness to learn from the experiences of others.

www.ingramcontent.com/pod-product-compliance
Lightning Source LLC
Chambersburg PA
CBHW071119220526
45467CB00004B/1965